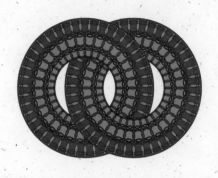

THE FORK WITHOUT HUNGER
poems **LAURIE LAMON**

THE FORK WITHOUT HUNGER
poems **LAURIE LAMON**

CavanKerry ❖ Press LTD.

CavanKerry Press Ltd.
Fort Lee, New Jersey
www.cavankerrypress.org

Library of Congress Cataloging-in-Publication Data
Lamon, Laurie, 1956–
  The fork without hunger : poems / by Laurie Lamon.— 1st ed.
     p. cm.
  ISBN 0-9723045-5-X (alk. paper)
  I. Title.

PS3612.A5474F67 2005
811'.6–dc22

                                          2004026739

Cover Art by Joseph Hart © 2004
Author Photograph by William Siems
Cover and book design by Peter Cusack

First Edition
Printed in the United States of America

I am greatly indebted to the Arnold S. Graves and Lois S. Graves Award in the Humanities, Whitworth College, and the Weyerhaeuser Center for Faith and Learning for their support during the period when many of these poems were written. I am particularly indebted to Tammy Reid, Bill Robinson, Lynn Noland, Dale Soden, and James Waller. I would like to gratefully acknowledge the personal encouragement and support of friends and colleagues Marty and Dave Erb, Doug and Linda Sugano, Nadine Chapman, Vic and Cathy Bobb, Laura Bloxham, Pamela Corpron Parker and Rob Parker, Linda and Jim Hunt, Lisa Sem-Rodrigues, and Leonard Oakland. I extend special gratitude for Martin Lammon's and Peter Davison's support and encouragement. I am deeply thankful to Donald Hall for his encouragement, his friendship, and his commitment to the heart and body of the poem.

CavanKerry Press is grateful for the support it receives from the New Jersey State Council on the Arts.

Acknowledgments

Grateful acknowledgment is made to the editors of the following journals in which these poems first appeared:

Arts & Letters Journal of Contemporary Culture: "Pain Tries to Think of Something," "Pain Thinks of Addressing the Body," "Pain Thinks of the Beautiful Table" (included also in *Pushcart XXVI*, Fall 2002), "Lithograph, *Sun Rising,* by Su Xin-Ping"

The Atlantic Monthly: "When You Tell Me," "Potato", "Praise" (included also in *180 More Extraordinary Poems for Every Day)*

The Colorado Review: "Pain Thinks of Achilles," "Pain Thinks of Longevity"

Cream City Review: "Pastoral"

The New Criterion: "Separating the Flowers"

The New Republic: "Night," "Pain Thinks of the Garden," "Pain Thinks of the Hand"

Northwest Review: "Poem"

Parnassus Literary Journal: "Garlic"

Ploughshares: "You Think of the Loss of Paradise," "Pain Thinks of the First Thing"

Poetry Northwest: "Ice Storm," "Pain Thinks of History," "The Day," "Twin," "Spectral"

Primavera: "Illness," "Killing the Dog"

Rock & Sling: "Olive, Plum," "Don't Speak to Me Now"

Southern Humanities Review: "Hummingbird"

Willow Springs: "Pain Thinks of Helen"

for William

It must be visible or invisible,
Invisible or visible or both:
A seeing and unseeing in the eye.

— from Wallace Stevens,
Notes toward a Supreme Fiction

The Fork Without Hunger

Foreword by Donald Hall   xiii

one

Pain Tries to Think of Something	3
Pain Thinks of History	5
Pain Thinks of Addressing the Body	6
White	7
Killing the Wasp	8
Illness	9
Garlic	10
Killing the Dog	11
Ice Storm	14
Demeter	16

two

Pain Thinks of Zero	19
Pain Thinks of the First Thing	20
Pain Thinks of the Hand	21
Don't Speak to Me Now	22
Olive, Plum	23
Poem	24
Night	25
When You Tell Me	26
Pastoral	27
Twin	29
Separating the Flowers	30

three

Pain Thinks of Achilles   33

Pain Thinks of Helen   34

Pain Thinks of Longevity   35

Spectral   36

You Think of the Loss of Paradise   37

Window   38

Ordinary Beauty   39

The Day   40

Praise   41

Hummingbird   42

Potato   43

Lithograph, *Sun Rising*, by Su Xin-Ping   44

Coda

Pain Thinks of Keeping Something   47

Pain Thinks of the Garden   48

Pain Thinks of the Beautiful Table   49

Foreword

There is such "Ordinary Beauty" in Laurie Lamon's pages, to use the title of her poem. *The Fork Without Hunger* is a book that takes continual joy in the natural world. Yet throughout these luxuriant lyrics physical pain runs like an underground river. Pain is unpunctuated, a constant presence, a motion under the earth's surface—but that surface is cherished. As ever, poetry happens, or reaches its uttermost, in the human collisions of contrary feeling. Torment twists in an oscillation of opposing currents—celebrations of flowers and dogs, of love and loss. When the dog is going to die, the poet leans back, "watching / the leaves of the flame-willow burn, the perishable / spring sap rising."

The poems render the experience of subtraction. So many expend the world into a fine point which vanishes into nothingness, a peace after the mess and entanglement of pain's world. As important as "nothing" is "without." When "Pain thinks of the Garden" it is "without memory / of birth without history without / moonlight …." Some of Lamon's landscapes are like still lives, a wonderful bright simplicity of apple and skull. Page after page, line after line, Lamon's language retains its purity, its chastity, its precision. ("Nothing but a garden dies with such accuracy….") The poet is attentive to cadences and line breaks, expertly gathering, pausing, and hurtling. There are improvisations of structure, like "I forget" in "Ice Storm," which organize a poem's strength and import.

Her poems are rare in their perfection of epithet, their delicacy of design, their cadence of attack. Take "Separating the Flowers":

> I rinsed the stems
> and lifted the dead blossoms
> from those still palpable
>
> with color and scent,
> then set the vase down again
> like a scale whose one side,

unburdened, rises.
The tiger lily lasted another
week. Lifting it, I thought

of Demeter and Mary
outlasting what must have felt,
at first, like desertion.

This poem is a triumph of concentrated cadence, the American language lovingly shaped and caressed, with its coda dependent on the reticent and scrupulous pause of "at first." Desertion and desolation remain at issue, Greek sweetness and Hebrew light together. Color and scent persist, the palpable blossoms.

— Donald Hall

one

Pain Tries to Think of Something

Ties a string around one finger.
Places a stone in each shoe. Stuffs
its clothes with paper,

watches sleeves catch and smoke.
Rubs its knees together, feeling
nerves flare. Tries to think

of literature physics shopping
malls lighted all night cups
of milk it exhorts its children

to drink every morning combing
their hair and attaching each
neckline's bitten hook and eye.

The children finish their juice
and cereal and try to guess
what animal what shape what color

is next while Pain weeps,
imagining an elephant hiding its bird-
like face in the trees.

At night while the children
sleep Pain thinks of the last thing,
watching the moon-

monument rise, then thinks
of something else, the body's mud
and straw crouched beneath stars.

Pain Thinks of History

Pulling its arms to its rib cage Pain thinks
of a sea horse small as a fern thinks of ladders

and tombs thinks of ruin's architecture
the vertebra's neural arch the torn net the artifact

Pain thinks of history without landscape without
bone or infinitive Pain thinks of the cordoned papyrus

the first and last page Pain thinks of the cell's
enormity sliding open and shut Pain thinks of history

without darkness and digs without darkness
without garbage or marrow Pain digs without thinking

of digging and the hand and the wrist without history
and the bracelet child size Pain slides up its arm.

Pain Thinks of Addressing the Body

As you tear down the frozen
stalks, as you rake over the garden,

as you drain the fountain,
and at night, listening for the small

shapes of animals lunging
through snow—

you are not thinking of paradise.
Like you, I endure

as the season you love endures,
radiant and frozen.

White

If death has a color it is not
the color of root or iron, the winter-
limned field emptied of grain and stalk.

It is not the color of water and soil
my mother wrung from the cloth she wrapped
around the hand I used to hold the cat

down, washing one and then the other
draining eye. I pushed its body
to the table and pried its jaw open for the eye-

dropper of food and the pill ground
to powder white as milk the cat smelled
and would not take.

Nothing but a garden dies with such accuracy,
I told my husband in April, reading
the instructions for water and coverage

from the bags of sterilized imported
soil he was mixing into the ground. He did not
hear me. He was breaking each seedling

down to the solid inch of bound
root white as the eye's geography pain
sees, entering the world.

Killing the Wasp

The hive was in the basement
wall. Each day I shook the drab
small workers, stunned by dark
in August, from the laundry pile—

or, coming down the stairs, I
met the larger wasps flying up,
wavering like the sun-struck
glass they sought. Standing still
to kill another, then leaning

close to see its self, I gathered
what I could not feel of emptiness
and weight the body curled
around itself: residential, sweet.

Illness

My sister is sorting clothes
as though at a yard sale,

or I look up from my bed
and she is leaning over me.

Between us, illness gleams
like the hour at dusk

when sparrows return
to the locust, the mountain

ash, the imperceptible nests
built close to the trunk

where nothing will sway,
where nothing is astounded.

Garlic

First the papery
hide, then the twin
halves and slight
violet veins I follow
with paring knife,
angling the blade
to catch what soaks
into the cutting board.
It has nothing to do
with absolution,
this routine of hands—
first the shine of oil,
and then water.

Killing the Dog

1

I bathe and brush the dog
knowing that by 5 p.m.
he'll be put down.

The kitchen window's
shine confirms
the little we know

of dying.
The dog settles into my arms
and we lean back, watching

the leaves of the flame-
willow burn, the perishable
spring sap rising.

2

This is not the worst
that can happen. I am not
the mother or father
who attends a daughter's grave
each day in good weather,
carrying the toy, the lawn chair,
the book and coffee cup
across green slopes and white
stone markers.

This is not the worst
that can happen. I am not
the dying woman
who has asked for music
to be turned off, flowers
to be carried from the room.

3

I would have shown you
a river bank, a horse
grazing, a river.

You would have believed
summer, then autumn.
You would have believed

a tree's rings could open
white as smoke after the tree
had been felled and cut

for the next season
and then carried into a room
where a fire burns and someone

is reading, or thinking of bed
where the husband or wife is
already asleep. Your meager shape

would have warmed them
until they returned to each other
in the morning, laying together

for a moment before rising
and placing their feet on each
cold side of the bed.

Ice Storm

I forget the cold bed's cargo of blankets, clothes,
candles in boxes whose Hallmark seals I break
with my thumb. I forget the dream of the boy and girl
wrapped in newspaper, and the father climbing
the city's Goodwill building. I forget his gray corduroy
pants. I forget his ankles and wrists. I forget the shovel,
the tire, the thermos of hot water. I forget Alkaline's
$5.00 rebate. I forget parking lots and MasterCard.

I forget shoppers lifting turkeys
and red tins of fruit cake; I forget fluorescent
lights and my neighbor's wave from the aisle
of imported food. I forget hair clips and the nape
of my neck. I forget lipstick and shopping
lists. I forget the woman at Hallmark when I ask
if I should buy fewer candles, leaving

candles for the woman behind me. I forget
the young wife on her way to the magazine aisle.
I forget that I was a wife. I forget the furnace, the desk,
the smell of garlic and tarragon, the vodka's
lime I lick and then my fingers. I forget the last 10,000
houses without power. I forget the birthday party,
the generator warming the house next door.
I forget the view fallen open of alley and windows,

the neighbor eye-level in his lighted rec room.
I forget the sound of the generator. I forget his wheelchair.
I forget my mother's farmhouse, the metal roof

where ice slides, blocking the door.
I forget the rancher, the condominium, the mobile home
where a couple dies heating the one long room
with charcoal. I forget charcoal and the grate where meat
burns. I forget to listen to the news. I forget

the snapped line meeting the ground;
I forget the workman who never saw it. I forget his name
and the names of his children. I forget the date
of his birth. I forget my niece asleep in her cotton sleeper.
I forget her crayons, and the cat warming herself
for an hour in sunlight. I forget sunlight.
I forget thousands of trees, and birds eating red berries.
I forget the gingko and the burlap ball of roots

I lifted, five years ago, into the trunk of my car.
I forget the gold collar of leaves circling the tender
joint of trunk and earth. I forget the shape
of my hand when I gather and drop fan-shaped leaves.
I forget identical cells inside identical veins.
I forget September and October. I forget the ground
beneath ice, the aspen bent to the ground where
I must crouch to enter and leave this house.

Demeter

In January you saw
the bulbs buried in darkness;

you heard the rustle
of dead leaves, the cells

breaking through soil and ice.
You waited, winter's

midwife, walking from room
to room, tending the fires.

two

Pain Thinks of Zero

who wants to lie down against earth once
without touching domain's perimeter
side & circumference the future
measured the interminable radius halved
Pain thinks of zero without parallel
nothing conjoined no offspring no line
where line ends after nothing Pain thinks
of the eye's constellation the earth
without emptiness Pain thinks of zero
without emptiness humming and void

Pain Thinks of the First Thing

without sleep without history the first thing
without sound without memory of sound

Pain thinks of origin's trespass *hoof* and *cochlea*
earth without blossom without axis

or column the Yangtze without passage the sea
without apparition and the animals let loose

at Peloponnesus Pain thinks of the first thing
without temple water black as burial's

locust and palm without fruit without water
Pain thinks of the first thing and drinks it

Pain Thinks of the Hand

without soil without light without
thumb or ash without food Pain thinks
of the hand without weight without
blossom or snow without Psalm Pain
thinks of blossom & Psalm without
day & night without translucence
Pain thinks of the hand without close
the pale cup the body's deluge

Don't Speak to Me Now

Over the wide waters
of rain, I hear you.
Through the incessant
corridor of air that follows
the stairway's hand-
rail up and down, morning
and night, I hear you.

Don't speak to me now.
Don't call my name.
I have been pulling weeds,
twisting the seedheads
weighted with stems,
following the descent into
each small conflagration
of root. Digging them up,
I bury again the dead I have
not begun to forget.

Olive, Plum

This morning as I closed the door,
the scent of plum

again, after twelve months—
the cool weirs of blossom like snow

falling, or the earth breaking
from stones on a hillside planted

with olive trees, the multitude
faithful to one season of light.

Poem

She notices the mirror
behind the table, the roses
gleaming like pieces

of china she has dropped
into a paper bag, then
the careful sweeping

of shards, and afterward
her hands searching
the floorboards.

Night

Nothing loves the spine. Breath is far
and cold, a window's fat

eye rising to the edge of lawn,
a pyracantha's weight of thorn and berry.

From inside the room, nothing looks like
reflection; it is us that separates light's

parts and whole into the sum we cannot
hold, lying side by side, our bodies

closing our mind's eye. Now it is us refusing
shine. Now it is us that is missing.

When You Tell Me

When you tell me I
should keep the house
and furniture, the air
inside the car is like
the breath a woman holds,
breaking eggs against
a bowl or listening
for the sound of shoes
in the bedroom, the closet
door closing where her
husband has just
stood, choosing a tie.

Pastoral

I am tired of the dog
wanting me
to run as he runs

through the yard's cold
channels you or I
shoveled again.

I am tired of the birds
in the mountain ash
and the berries

fallen early last fall,
reappearing
now in January's false

spring through late
falling snow that melts
and freezes again.

I remember placing
my hands
in leather gloves,

touching each
fallen plum without
ceremony

in August, rolling
each plum back and forth
before picking it up

and the wasp
curled inside, kneeling
and drinking.

Twin

Not her voice, not snow
covering stones. Not the glasses of milk she drank.
Not the shape of her mouth.

For years, made to sleep in one bed,
we watched light break the room into edges

our hands learned to follow
like the nightgowns we pulled, curled on our sides,

down over our feet.
We knew that the world would end with light,

that pain would inhabit the body,
that the mind would forget its one resemblance.

Separating the Flowers

I rinsed the stems
and lifted the dead blossoms
from those still palpable

with color and scent,
then set the vase down again
like a scale whose one side,

unburdened, rises.
The tiger lily lasted another
week. Lifting it, I thought

of Demeter and Mary
outlasting what must have felt,
at first, like desertion.

three

Pain Thinks of Achilles

the immeasurable cold drawn up without distance noon without
wind Pain tears with its feet climbing down the day's billowing wall
witnessing animals without harness the dead without burial Pain
weights the garden with plastic and stone and listens across water
through soil farther through darkness than Muta in Tartarus hearing
the last space the eye closes and Pain already beyond it

Pain Thinks of Helen

watching the sea and the yards of sand flat as her thumb
writing letters for sixty years what next what year assigned

whose face without rapture's addiction what fact growing old
Menelaus covers their daughter at night folding her t-shirts

packing the apple and sandwich thinking of beauty's last trace
last deal best price at the end of the war Pain rubs the backs

of the dead rubs smoke from the sky inscribing their names
into the book where their names appear day after day

Pain thinks of famine's children thronging the street Pain
thinks of Helen reading headlines closing the closet door visiting

tombs crematoriums palatial as light's origin whose brilliant stones
she climbs kissing the husband gone early to bed kissing

the daughter asleep for hours her fingers pulled to her mouth
the stuffed toy dragged through the bars

Pain Thinks of Longevity

wind lifting wave the world without interference
tonnage and dialogue flourishing Pain watches
space taper and end dark as molecules' atoms water
and salt Pain travels south and then north studying
sand in the first place stone beaten to petrified
animal chipped from its shell Pain studies unfolding
the region's map the next thing soundless below
the sea's province Pain thinks of dropping money
into the view master waiting for whales to breach
Pain thinks of the solid world the vast disturbances

Spectral

Look up, my husband said.
If we were in a twelfth-century play,
this show of light
would have something to do with us
and God—

Look up, he said, as if to make
apparent what we think
is ordinary: sequence of shadow
and branch, darkness
and light, light without mercy.

You Think of the Loss of Paradise

When you stood up and walked past the rows
of desks and windows whose yellow and green

trees you had already admired, praising even the door
where you had stood before entering,

imagining yourself reading passages of sin or love
or the earth or moon's ashen birth—

what amazement you must have felt
later, looking back down the sunlit aisle

to the blackboard, chalk-marked and dry as a cough
the body tires of, tired of nature's aging

catastrophe—you were right to think of the loss
of paradise, on the street folding the ends

of your scarf against your ears so that you could hear
yourself singing, so the tongue's nomenclature

could mean nothing else: not the end
of the century, not the sea's dazzle and hieroglyphs

still beckoning, not the roar of traffic
or the language of signs ground into the dim scene's

capacity for light and darkness. Not darkness.
Not the wind that was there.

Window

I waved while you backed the car into the alley
and waited as you saw that I watched,
that I moved from doorway to window, looking
through the locust branches to the place
you were leaving, turning left onto the street
and looking back until the house and the yard
were gone, until the space between us closed
like the window where I no longer was, and time
with its jaw brushing the ground went on
smelling the churn of dirt and oil, went on tracking
the tread of our shoes, our cars, a thousand
times the taste of nothing, the taste of no memory.

Ordinary Beauty

We are without history, we are
unfallen, holding each other,

traversing the hotel path, trying
to imagine a time before we

remember having seen it—
then one of us saying, "Look,

look at the sea," and watching
it rise and fall into one body

without beginning or end,
without knowledge of radiance

or shade, morning or shattering
noon, without cessation

the sea covering earth
like a hand placed over the heart.

The Day

Turning onto our street, I watch for the lights
    we left on this morning, and think how the darkness,
        arriving ahead of us, is spectacular

as the leaf one of us will track into the house this evening,
    carrying the mail or bringing the dog,
        not seeing how the yard has drifted

closed, or the perilous flights of birds from cold
    nest to cold ground, the snow melting and freezing
        on porch steps by early afternoon.

Closing my office door, I was not thinking of the living room
    window bare of reflection where children
        glance, walking from school.

I was not thinking of the drive ahead of me, or you,
    or the music, a Renaissance harp, I would hear as traffic
        slowed and snow iced the windshield

hours ago, by now
    having noticed the leaf shard's gleam like an animal's
        eye, looking up—

by now having leaned close to catch the broken edge
    with a fingernail, and seeing the stratum
        and multitude.

Praise

I heard the dogs before
I opened the door late, after work—
first Maude who was dancing
in praise of my arrival for all she knew
it was: presence without end,
the end of waiting, the end
of boredom—
                    and then Li Po,
who, in the middle of his life,
learning to make his feelings known
as one who has carried breath
and heart close to the earth seven
times seven years, in praise
of silence and loneliness, climbed
howling, howling from his bed.

Hummingbird

Yesterday as I watered the garden,
      a hummingbird held itself so near
            my hand I could see its body's

closed parentheses, feel against
      my arm the place where it turned,
         poised in the spray

where it must have bathed
      or drunk, and where, afterward,
           passing

my hand through
      the changed air, I could feel
         nothing.

Potato

There is one beauty
it knows. The rest is blindness,
earth closing around itself,
surrounded by hunger.

For a hundred days,
a thousand, it is the same
dark eye looking
inward. Thinking of light.

Remembering the pressure
of soil. The seam
of water finding its heart.
And afterward,

blossoms ringing through
stone.

Lithograph, *Sun Rising*, by Su Xin-Ping

A man
greets first light,
light

apparent on brow
and headcloth,
the shirt draping

hip and knee.
His wrists turn
the palms out

the way a woman
knows
with her hands

the back
of a man sleeping,
knows wind

in the garden,
having
carried the lanterns.

Coda

Pain Thinks of Keeping Something

artifact or weight the gray hair the hallway's
shoe & sound of instrument or light

bending without sound or measurement
Pain thinks of keeping something the body's

silhouette sun-struck the hand
perennial as stem Pain thinks of keeping

something the field the repetition of field
the black bell the memory of bells

Pain Thinks of the Garden

without breath without distance
puffed and curled without sanctuary
or altar's wine without bread
without orchid or dust Pain thinks
of the body without memory
of birth without history without
moonlight entering the garden
darkening the trees and the statuary
the body's grieving shoulders

Pain Thinks of the Beautiful Table

the way water looks up Pain thinks of the beautiful table
surrounded by light Pain thinks of glass & cup iridescence
& afterwards paper & mouth the wall Pain is used to craving
the hand lifting the usual thing Pain thinks of the body's
meekness the fork without hunger without interruption Pain
thinks of going for days without the beautiful table without
food or expression so that flowers & cold are drawn in